PRAISE FOR ADAM RAPP AND *NOCTURNE*

"There is an undeniable, cumulative power to the writing here."　　　　　—Bruce Weber, *The New York Times*

"At once beautiful and haunting, compelling and agonizing . . . A bold, elegant and even funny exploration of how a single moment has the power both to connect us and change our lives."

—Mark de la Viña, *San Jose Mercury News*

"Tragically eloquent . . . Rapp [is] a writer with a unique voice who is a master of poetic realism."

—Patti Hartigan, *The Boston Globe*

"I can't wait to see what [Rapp] will do next. His text is lushly poetic, full of the kind of quirky detail you'll find in Cormac McCarthy or William Gaddis."

—David Cote, *Time Out New York*

"Rapp . . . is an ambitious and prodigiously talented writer."

—Charles Isherwood, *Variety*

"The language is almost obscenely voluptuous."
—Steven Winn, *San Francisco Chronicle*

"Achingly beautiful." —Terry Byrne, *Boston Herald*

"There's no denying the power and poignancy of Rapp's prose." —Robert Dominguez, New York *Daily News*

"This undeniable talent with the pitch-dark new voice has a way with the exorable force of cumulative grief."
—Linda Winer, *Newsday*

"Lyrical and surreal . . . Rapp's language has an acute, corporeal life of its own." —Carolyn Clay, *The Boston Phoenix*

ADAM RAPP

NOCTURNE

Adam Rapp has been the recipient of the 1997 Herbert
& Patricia Brodkin Scholarship; a fellowship to the Ca-
margo Foundation in Cassis, France; two Lincoln Center
LeComte du Nouy Awards; the 1999 Princess Grace Award
for Playwriting; the 2000 Roger L. Stevens Award from the
Kennedy Center Fund for New American Plays; a 2000
Suite Residency with Mabou Mines; and the 2001 Helen
Merrill Award for Emerging Playwrights. His plays have
been produced at Victory Gardens in Chicago, The 24th
Street Theatre in Los Angeles, The Juilliard School, The
American Repertory Theatre in Cambridge, Massachu-
setts, Berkeley Repertory, New York Theatre Workshop,
and the Bush Theatre in London. A graduate of Clarke
College in Dubuque, Iowa, he also completed the Lila
Acheson Wallace Playwriting Fellowship at Juillard.

Nocturne was awarded Boston's Elliot Norton Award for Best New Script as well as Best New Play by the Independent Reviewers of New England. It was chosen as one of the ten "Best Plays of 2000–2001" (the annual Chronicle of U.S. theater).

Rapp is also the author of the novels *Missing the Piano*, *The Buffalo Tree*, and *The Copper Elephant*. He lives in New York City.

NOCTURNE

FABER AND FABER, INC.

An affiliate of Farrar, Straus and Giroux / New York

NOCTURNE

a play by

ADAM RAPP

FABER AND FABER, INC.
An affiliate of Farrar, Straus and Giroux
19 Union Square West, New York 10003

Copyright © 2001 by Adam Rapp
All rights reserved
Distributed in Canada by Penguin Books of Canada Limited
Printed in the United States of America
FIRST EDITION, 2002

Grateful acknowledgment is given for permission to reprint lyrics from
Steely Dan's "Hey Nineteen," written by Donald Fagen and Walter
Becker. © 1980 Freejunket Music (ASCAP)/Zeon Music (ASCAP). All
rights reserved. International copyright secured.

Library of Congress Cataloging-in-Publication Data
Rapp, Adam.
    Nocturne : a play / by Adam Rapp.— 1st ed.
        p.   cm.
    ISBN 0-571-21132-1 (alk. paper)
    1. Accident victims—Family relationships—Drama.
2. Fathers and sons—Drama.   3. New York (N.Y.)—Drama.
4. Joliet (Ill.)—Drama.   5. Young men—Drama.   I. Title.

PS3568.A6278 N63 2002
812'.54—dc21

                                        2001053151

No performance or reading of this work may be given without express
permission of the author. Inquiries regarding amateur and stock
performance rights should be addressed to: Broadway Play Publishing,
56 East 81st Street, New York, New York, 10028-0202, (212) 772-8334,
fax (212) 772-8358. For all other rights contact the author's agent:
Carl Mulert, The Joyce Ketay Agency, 1501 Broadway, Suite 1908,
New York, New York 10036, (212) 354-6825.

Author photograph copyright © 2000 by Steven Freeman

Designed by Gretchen Achilles

www.fsgbooks.com

1   3   5   7   9   10   8   6   4   2

FOR SARAH

ACKNOWLEDGMENTS

The author would like to thank Brad Rouse, Carl Mulert, Marsha Norman, Dallas Roberts, Marcus Stern, Elizabeth Reaser, Walt Niedner, and especially Bob Brustein.

—Yes *he thought* Between grief and nothing I will take grief.

—WILLIAM FAULKNER, *The Wild Palms*

NOCTURNE

Nocturne received its world premiere on October 15, 2000, at the American Repertory Theatre in Cambridge, Massachusetts, and was developed with the generous support of the Harold and Mimi Steinberg Charitable Trust and the Carr Foundation. The play was first produced in New York on May 4, 2001, by the New York Theatre Workshop in collaboration with the American Repertory Theatre, with Robert Brustein (A.R.T.) and Jim Nicola (NYTW) as Artistic Directors.

Nocturne was directed by Marcus Stern. The scenic design was by Christine Jones, costume design by Viola Mackenthun, lighting design by John Ambrosone; sound design was by Marcus Stern and David Remedios. The Production Stage Manager was Jennifer Rae Moore. The cast was as follows:

THE SON	Dallas Roberts
THE SISTER	Nicole Pasquale
JAN, THE MOTHER	Candice Brown
EARL, THE FATHER	Will LeBow
THE REDHEADED GIRL WITH THE GRAY-GREEN EYES	Marin Ireland

CHARACTERS

THE SON, thirty-two

THE SISTER, eight

JAN, THE MOTHER, mid-forties

EARL, THE FATHER, mid-forties/early sixties

THE REDHEADED GIRL WITH THE GRAY-GREEN EYES,
mid-twenties

I

Fifteen years ago I killed my sister.

There.

I said it.

I can change the order of the words. My sister I killed
fifteen years ago. I, fifteen years ago, killed my sister.
Sister my killed I years ago fifteen.

I can cite various definitions. To deprive of life: The
farmer killed the rabid dog. To put an end to: The umpire
killed the tennis match. To mark for omission: He killed
the paragraph. To destroy the vital essential quality of:
The dentist killed the nerve with Novocain. To cause to
stop: The bus driver killed the engine. To cause extreme
pain to: His monologue killed the audience.

To slay. To murder. To assassinate. To dispatch. To execute.

You can play with tenses. Will kill. Did kill. Have killed. Will have killed. Would like to have killed.

You can turn it into a gerund. Killing.

There's a kind of progress with a gerund.

If you conjugate in the past tense, it's all the same. I killed. You killed. He, she, it killed. They killed. You all killed. We killed. There's no way around it.

Fifteen years ago I killed my sister.

It's dumb-sounding, the way most facts are. Like a former President or the names of bones.

Grover Cleveland.

Fibula. Tibia. Femur.

There's a finality in a fact. Something medical almost. A fact is crafted. Vaguely industrial. It has permanence. It's a stain or a smudge. A botch or a spot or a blemish. A fact is a flaw. It's made of wood and left to fossilize; to gather minerals and geologically imprint itself on the side of a mountain.

You can look at the back of your hand and know exactly how the bones move.

(The sound of a distant piano.)

The piano doesn't sing. It sobs. It aches without release. Like a word that can't wrench itself from the throat. Like an alkaline trapped in the liver. Even one note. A C-sharp. The death of small bird. An F. A stranded car's horn bleating for help on the highway. The piano has permanence. A factual permanence. You walk into a room and there it is, in all its stoic grandeur. It has omnipotence. It waits for you without pursuit. The hulking, coffinlike stillness. The way it comes to know your touch. Like a lover's private indulgence. A kind of glacial intimacy. A cold, sexless knowing.

Grieg. Chopin. Tchaikovsky.

There's a kind of death with the piano. The final note falling. Perhaps it's the inevitable, ensuing silence. The deafening return to stillness. The instrument itself is a homicide waiting to happen. Its physical weight. Its gravity, which slows you. The seeming need it has to render you inert. To turn you into its motionless companion. As though it *doesn't* want to be played. As though its potential—the crushing unheard music—as though this absence alone is some kind of motion deterrent.

The final movement of a sonata. An almost-human tragedy. Slow, brutal heart failure. Coronary thrombosis.

The weaving voices interloping a fugue. A political death. A kind of vocal assassination.

Fifteen years ago I killed my sister.

I was seventeen, she was nine. A fact. Now I'm thirty-two. She would be twenty-four. Fact. The hipbone's connected to the leg bone.

The '69 Buick Electra 225 is a very lengthy car. There's something almost illegal about the expanse of its back end. From grille to taillight it's sixteen feet, nine inches long. It has a 440 engine, and when you accelerate you can feel the horsepower buzzing in your ribcage. It's like a car out of a comic book.

At my father's insistence, I buy the Electra from Bob Ranzini—our family's insurance broker—for two hundred and fifty bucks. Mr. Ranzini pats me on the back. He brags of its classic American pedigree. He speaks of its great sluicing hum and his yearly drive down to Jupiter, Florida, and all the old two-lane highways in the South.

Sitting in the Electra is like lounging. There's this sense that platters of food will be served. The seats buzz back. The windows buzz down. This infinite buzzing. Like the invisible drone of bees at work. Locusts in the fruit trees. A car humming with electricity.

The accident happens like this:

Joliet, Illinois. I'm coming home from Sub-Diggity—my summer sandwich-making job. I'm seventeen. I'm just off work. My clothes smell like roast beef and mayonnaise. My fingers are stained with mustard. Steely Dan's "Hey Nineteen" is playing on the AM.

(Singing)

Way back when
In sixty-seven

I was the dandy
Of Gamma Chi

I'm traveling west on Black Road. There is no wind. The air is so hot it folds in through the window like an invisible quilt. It slouches into the passenger seat. After being on my feet for eight hours I'm not exactly in my body. I'm somewhere else; somewhere near the music. Under the words. The bass line's all liquid velvet. It's a cool creamy liquor, this bass line.

It's the second week in July. It's roughly 95 degrees. Mosquitoes are plotting their midsummer feast. Moths are hovering under the gas station sign in a great epileptic nimbus. There's an endless feeling of Little League being played. Nocturnally and with infinite concessions. Slurpies and caramel corn. Blue snow cones staining the chins of toddlers. Hot dogs that are so good they can feed entire families. An ocean of Little League diamonds.

An aluminum bat hitting a ball is one of the greatest notes of July. A D, I think. A split-second song. A little chink of hope.

I turn north onto Gael Drive.

(Singing)

Sweet things from Boston
So young and willing
Moved down to Scarsdale
Where the hell am I?

I'm going 45 in a 30. At least that's where the speedometer
freezes after the collision. I like to call it a collision,
because decapitation sounds somehow capital.
Corporeal.

We've lived on Gael Drive for most of my life. My mother,
Jan; my father, Earl; and my little sister and I. It's a three-
bedroom ranch house with blond brick. We have a garage
and a sprinkler system. We have a birdhouse. We have
dragonflies that hover and dart like miniature helicopters.
We have bees. We have a small bearded gnome that looks
as if he's suffering from some sort of gastrointestinal
disorder. In the front yard there's a sycamore tree that
bleeds. At night its shadow hangs on my bedroom window
like an enormous man trembling.

Inside the house we have infinite Formica. Bookshelves
and cupboards and countertops. Tables and sideboards.

Desks and dressers and headboards all around. A credenza. There's so much Formica it's as if it was archaeologically excavated and the house was built around it in honor of its laminated magnificence.

I sometimes think that the color of my skin is not white but Formica.

In the living room we have a 1942 Steinway piano. There is not a scratch on it. It's my father's prize possession. It was his father's—Grandpa Earl—and it was handed down with the understanding that it would be played only if the hands that traveled its ivory cusps were worthy of its glory. My father would spend hundreds of dollars having it tuned every spring.

In our blond house the Steinway is so black it sometimes has an air of war. As though it can be mounted and fired up and driven right through the Sheetrock. My mother places doilies on its hood and family pictures on the doilies. My dad holding a rather bored-looking bass. My sister in a pair of roller skates that make her prepubescent legs look long and coltish. My parents clutching each other at the altar, looking as if they're about to walk into a meat locker. An 8-by-10 seventh-grade photo of me.

Snaggletoothed. My hair trying to levitate in one very large and rollicking cowlick.

I would play that Steinway from the ages of ten to seventeen. I would practice for three hours a day and I would play until my hands would grow long and slender like a woman's. I would eventually start walking around hunched and knotted like some kind of Transylvanian harpsichordist. My parents would enter me into local competitions, where mothers and fathers execute a cold, Machiavellian reticence. Sitting together not as husbands and wives but as co-conspirators. Not as lovers but as collaborators in the industry of manufacturing perfection. Hands poised on knees. Backs arched. Necks stiff with righteous perpendicularity. Some stand incredibly still, as though their severity will somehow conjure the perfect note. Some kneel in a strange, sustained genuflection. Some position themselves in the aisles, arms akimbo. A posture of gentle warfare.

These parents are agents and coaches and tutors and mentors and managers all rolled into one. They are priest and jailer. Savior and executioner. Investor. They lock you in practice rooms and surreptitiously record your third crack at Grieg. They keep time with a pencil better than your teacher. They drill you and hug you and make you manicure your nails to the point of cuticle supremacy. It is uncompromising, willful training.

Over time a horse owner rears his prize colt from foal to derby winner with the subtle sustained use of his riding crop.

I would win some of the small competitions. I would lose all of the big ones.

So, it's seven-thirty and the sun is a flaming orb on the horizon. There are colors in the sky. Reds. Pinks. Burnt oranges. Clouds like frayed gauze. Their underbellies golden somehow.

Steely Dan is well into its chorus.

(Singing)

The Cuervo gold
The fine Colombian
Make tonight a wonderful thing
Say it again . . .

I turn north onto Gael Drive and I decide to not go home. There's a place where I sometimes go and think. It's an enormous platoon of power lines that buzz with a kind of indifferent somnolence. The Radio Trees. Some people go to bars. Others go to the quarry. Some go to a restaurant on the East Side where women in cheap lingerie will dance on your table. I go to the Radio Trees. I want to take my shoes off and feel the buzz in my feet.

I accelerate. Something small runs out into the road. I brake. Nothing happens. It's a dog. A garbage can. A plastic bag that's stolen a bit of breeze. I pump the brake pedal. I might as well be pumping a bologna sandwich. I swerve. There's a thud. A hollow, almost wooden thud. Small as an egg. I continue pumping the brakes. Nothing happens. Steely Dan turns into the Alan Parsons Project. I am the eye in the sky. I pump the brakes and the Electra just keeps going, as though by its own volition. I swerve. I counterswerve. I crash into a large oak tree at the end of the street. The front end of the Electra accordions to the windshield. Birds are everywhere. A schizophrenic cloud of crows.

I crack three ribs and break my nose. I can taste the metal in my blood. Like warm pewter. The speedometer sticks at 45 miles per hour.

In that strange, post-crash ethereal silence I get out of the car and walk the hundred yards or so back to where I heard the thud. The crows have formed a kind of wavering anvil and are flying south toward the sound of the highway. It feels as if the steering wheel has been inserted into my rib cage. My legs take me. The hipbone is connected to the leg bone.

My sister's body lies in the street. It looks like a doll's body. Legs. Feet. Yellow socks perfectly folded. Bits of lace turned down—my mother's touch. Shoes so small it's as if they were born out of a children's fable. Hands. Arms. Neck. A small white dress with blue flowers. Anemones. Buttercups.

Her head is across the street. It has rolled into the Petersens' driveway. I walk over and pick it up. Simply. Perfunctorily. Only a feeling of great clarity and absence. Like a sudden gust of lake wind. As if it's a ball or some kind of fugitive picnic toy. Its weight seems tremendous. I will reattach it to the neck and she will rise off the pavement and go back into the house and wash up for supper.

As I'm reattaching, my mother can be seen framed in the living-room window, her hand pressed against the glass, her head slightly tilted, as though she is peering out over a strange body of water; as though she is watching something hellish emerging from the fog.

The sound of sirens. Shrieking sirens from all directions. The shrieking turns into a kind of weeping. Sirens weeping in an octave only known to whales and dolphins.

II

I can't remember my sister's face.

Other parts of her are as definite as forks and knives.

Her little blond knees. Legs so slender you wonder how they could support the weight of even the smallest torso. Her wrists as thin as Popsicle sticks. Her boyish arms. Mosquito-bitten. Stained with iodine and calamine lotion. Her tiny hands. Her fingers as light and delicate as bird bones. The moons in her nails. Their infinitesimal hemispheres. Some setting into the beds of her cuticles. Others rising as though coaxed by some kind of centrifugal song.

I can sometimes see the ears. Unusually large ears for a small girl. Lobes like dangling tears of putty. The ears of a barber or a train conductor. An odd, manly wisdom in those ears.

I try to reconstruct the images. In that strange, filmic method of the memory I use still frames. I break it down into celluloid. But before the storyboard there's the mood. The intangibles. The acceleration of the Electra. A kind of vague feeling of satisfaction wending through my intestines. The Radio Trees calling me. The steering wheel smelling of cold cuts. Steely Dan. The feeling of levitation, as though the tires are only on the road because of the constraints of physics. The heat curdling in the front seat. Radiating from the vinyl dash like a boiled medicine shirt that is drawn to the skin.

And then that flash and all those kaleidoscopic possibilities.

Frame 1: A dog; King—the Petersens' German shepherd.

Frame 2: A bird; a spooked swallow swooping down from some unknown eaves; nosediving into the grille at the threat of rain.

Frame 3: A small garbage can: green somehow, for recycling, and plastic, because there's no music in the thud.

Frame 4: A miskicked football hurtling end over end from the Doughertys' back yard.

And then Frame 5:

My sister in her dress; so clean it's as if she's been bathed in preparation for her portrait to be painted; her knees; the slightly ducklike pronation of her feet; ducklinglike, I should say; her saddle shoes; the yellow socks with lace; her white dress with the little flowers; the quality of white Roman somehow; the flowers so blue it's as if they are singing; her hand rising up theatrically.

Stop.

Please stop.

Not now.

Not like this.

I'm too small for this to happen.

Sure, I play with the drama. I tweak it. I raise and lower the hand. Palm out. Index finger extended toward the windshield accusatorially. I add and remove inflection. I see it as text and I italicize. I bold. I underscore to drive it home. I fold in shrieks and bogeyman screams and tears. Yes, tears. As if she even had time to well up.

I've plummeted to the depths of comedy. She'll wink at me. She'll have a handlebar mustache. She'll be holding a deck of cards, peel off the joker, frame it with her hand, and then fling it toward the windshield with ironic, magicianlike skill. She'll snicker and sneer. She'll pull out a small saddle horn and honk with great velocity. She'll chortle. She'll flimflam and rabble-rouse. She'll lift her dress and reveal a very loud set of rainbow suspenders.

The fact is that no matter how I reconstruct the instant of impact, the only thing that endures is an overwhelming blankness. A blip of nothing. Zero. A goose egg. As though the sound—that hollow thud—was a product of some kind of neighborhood ventriloquism. As if the asphalt itself was in vaudevillian cahoots with the Hardens or the Petersens.

She swam. She rode her bike. While I practiced for a conservatory audition, she sat under the piano bench and crayoned pictures of clowns with balloons in their cheeks.

She liked boys' clothes. She'd steal my boxer shorts and wear them to swimming practice. Once, at dinner, she ambitiously announced her plan of owning a tuxedo. She intended to wear it to her fourth-grade graduation.

My mother, of course, made her wear dresses and pierced her ears.

She proposed marriage to me at least once a week. She'd go to a knee and say, Marry me, you big juicy hunk of yummy boy steak. I'm not kidding. She'd actually say that. And then she'd laugh and I'd laugh, and the chorus of our laughter was like a jet flying through our silent blond house.

She imitated dogs. She would get down on all fours and howl at the siren from a distant fire truck. She would mime a spell of rather lengthy canine urination into a nook of the sofa. She'd mark her territory in virtually all corners of the house.

She called me Dorkus.

Once she pasted together thirty-seven of my baseball cards and put them under my pillow. I was furious.

So the memories are there. As clear as if they happened yesterday.

I just can't see her face.

Sometimes I actually picture two enormous X's stamped over her eyes. Something from the Sunday comics. I change her hair color on a daily basis. She was a rhubarb blonde. No, she wasn't, she was a redhead and she had tortellini-like curls. She had straight brown hair. She was bald. Her skull gleamed with a kind of lunar sorrow.

I wonder if she wanted to be hit. She wasn't chasing a ball or a kite. There weren't any kids calling to her from the other side of Gael Drive. She wasn't pushed from behind. No 30-mile-an-hour winds. Not a tornado reported within a hundred miles that day. From our driveway, approaching cars can be seen at least fifty yards away.

No, she wasn't abused. She wasn't ridiculed. She was rarely, if ever, sent to her room. She was loved. And fed. She was well clothed. She was the first girl on her swim team to do the butterfly. In jacks she was good to sixes. Her hands were quicker than mine ever were during the fastest

arpeggio. She tried to read Stephen King novels. She was
curious. My mother had to take *The Shining* away from her
three times.

A faceless child walks in front of a speeding car. I could
buy that. A man with three children and a beautiful wife
leaps from the thirtieth floor of his Wall Street building. A
pregnant woman walks off the Verrazano Bridge and
everyone says she was so happy. Hemingway sticks a rifle
in his mouth. Jerzy Kosinski asphyxiates himself with a
plastic bag and floats to his death in a bathtub. Even
in literature. Anna Karenina jumps in front of a train.
Lily Bart does it with chloroform. But you never hear
about it with children. It's always an accident. Trains and
buses. The parking lots at supermarkets. That one slippery
ledge at the quarry. Tragedy's poker. God's ugly deck of
cards.

Perhaps there is a kind of death wish in some children.
They see the grim vision from the window of their school
bus. The two-car garages. The gabled roofs and the
manicured lawns and the sedans just sitting there like
enormous, uninspired termites. I don't want to *be* an adult.
I don't want to *do* that. I don't want to hide behind the
drapes and darn my husband's socks and have my senses

deadened by the Freon-cooled whir of central air. I don't want my belly to distend with multiple pregnancies or the disease of tumors or the sediment of red meat. I don't want this stifling, suburban affliction. I don't even want pubic hair. I want to swim and run and spin. I want to get away with things. I want to eat snow cones for the rest of my life. I *like* my little blond knees, thank you very much. I have the right to keep them little and blond. So I'll end it while the going's still good. And I'll make it quick. I'll walk in front of a speeding car. It will be like walking to the edge of the high dive. I'll even take a bath and throw on my favorite dress first.

The evening of my sister's death it was discovered that the brake line on the Electra had snapped.

I'm in the hospital, floating through the cumulonimbus ether of some narcotic analgesic, when my mother walks—or rather glides—into my room like some kind of cigar-store Indian on casters.

I would say that Jan is and has always been a handsome woman. You read about handsome women in novels. I always envision Abraham Lincoln in an evening gown. Faulkner's women. Outliving the South as though they were born in the boughs of cottonwoods. You get the sense that when they reach the end of their lives they don't die but rather affect a kind of graceful expiration: a return to the woods, where their bones don't dwindle to dust but find roots in the ground and braid into the great hairy trees of the Delta. Even the beautiful Charlotte from *The Wild Palms*. The blue-collar artist. Always wearing men's pants. Her yellow eyes. Steinbeck's Depression-thickened matriarchs. All those journeying Joad women. Their bare feet as tough as canvas shoes. The young ones round-shouldered and prematurely varicosed from the labor of farming. Jan could have been a Joad. It's not that my mother doesn't indulge in the wearing of makeup or the Arctic-like frosting of her hair; she owns enough beauty products to slather down an entire police force. It's the jaw. The brow. The strong, squarish chin. Something wooden and angular. As though this structural strength is not from a quality found in the marrow of her cheekbones but, rather, like a hard, metallic property detected in a thing old and ossified; a condition like rust or fossilization; something that is perhaps present in floorboards that have been around since the Civil War. It's a thing beyond her German ancestry.

So my handsome mother enters the room. Her hair is so shellacked with sprays and balms and mousses that it looks like a kind of gentle furniture on her head. Her face hardened with grief. Her makeup so severe it looks as if she was forced to apply it at knife point. She sits in a chair beside me for a long time before she speaks. I look down and see that her hands are clenched into fists. Her nylon running suit periodically crackles like fire.

After a long, medical silence, she tells me about the brake line.

She says, "It was the brake line."

A nurse enters and checks something on my chart. She exits without a greeting or a goodbye.

My mother says, "They're going to let you off with involuntary manslaughter."

The word "man." The word "slaughter."

She says, "The only thing you are guilty of is failure to stop to avoid an accident."

She almost sounds disappointed.

––––––

A long, slow-motion gurney passes by my room. Despite the expanse of chrome and the spidering lines and the chutes and the tubes and its accompanying intravenous bladder that somehow looks like a crystal kidney proudly plucked and mounted in glorious, surgical crucifixion, the whole thing, with all its gleaming, prophylactic paraphernalia, is as noiseless as a twig floating in a stream. The patient in transit is missing her chin.

"A fifty-dollar fine," my mother says. "Your father paid it for you."

I say, "Tell him thanks."

She says, "He's taking it very hard."

There's a picture in my room of a little clown with balloons in her cheeks. A child clown holding an enormous, vulturous umbrella. It could have been something that my sister crayoned under the piano bench. I think this is a cruel joke. Somehow hospitals are designed to terrorize you with a benign, affectless contempt. In their cold, fluorescent indifference, recovery always carries with it a kind of haunting. Incontinence. Post-surgery hypothermia. The lung collapse of the body weaning itself from anesthesia. A picture of a small clown with balloons in her cheeks.

I say, "How are *you*, Mother?"

She doesn't respond. Her eyes are screaming to blink. The dehydrated whites broiled to a dull pink. They look like they'd be hot if you touched them.

I say, "I'm sorry, Mother."

She says, "It wasn't your fault."

I say, "I know, but still."

And then she says it again. She says, "Your father is taking it pretty hard."

I say, "Of course."

"But we'll get through this," she says.

Then we are silent for a while, and when I try to move, it feels as if there is crushed glass in my lungs. I cry out, and in that moment, my mother reaches her hand up. I think she is going to place it on my forehead. Or my cheek. But she halts. And her hand is suspended there. As though she is hailing a taxi. As though there is a sheet of boiling glass between us. And then she lowers her hand and it turns back into a fist in her lap.

"Rest well," she says. And then she gets up and walks out. The abrasion of her nylon running suit can be heard suspiring down the corridor in a small, hot whisper.

That would be the last thing my mother would say to me:

Rest well.

A month after the accident, she would move out of our little blond house on Gael Drive and into an apartment with her sister. She would live with my aunt for three years and then, one day, nearly eight years after having transplanted to New York—ironically the day I land a contract for my first novel—I receive a letter from her sister saying that my mother has been moved to a private boarding residence for the clinically depressed.

I would later learn of the daily diet of a hundred milligrams of Haldol and the bench where she spends most of her afternoons incessantly singing "Old MacDonald's Farm" and that her favorite pastime is the making of potholders.

That endless looping and weaving.

My father takes the death of my sister pretty hard. Earl is, or I should say *was*, the superintendent at the local junior high. Monge Junior High. My third day back from the hospital he calls me into his study. I'm not yet walking too well. With each step there's still that crushed glass to deal with.

We haven't spoken since I've been home. We've passed each other in the kitchen the way canoes pass in a lake; with a silent, dumb inevitability.

I hover at the door to his study, leaning against the jamb. He can't look at me. When he speaks it's with a kind of detached analog. His grief has turned him into a robot. He is Earl the Automaton.

He says, "Come in, Son."

I've lost my name. I've turned into that anonymous, boyish pronoun used by policemen and coaches: "Son." Which basically means "non-son." It feels as if he's going to make me clap erasers after school. He's going to give me an hour of detention.

I enter his study. It's as clean as a church. His computer issuing forth a vague blue light. The hard drive dog-whistling subliminally. *Encyclopedia Britannica* filling the first shelf of his bookcase in all its vertical propriety. Awards from the school district framed along the back wall. A small mariner's clock clipping time.

I sit across from him at his hulking oak banker's desk. His hands are flat on the blotter. His head tilted down, almost shamefully. There is a small snub-nosed revolver set between the axis of his thumbs. It looks like a young blackbird sleeping. I have never seen this gun before. I had no idea that there was a small black gun living in our small blond house.

When he finally looks up, his eyes are as wide as eggs.

I say, "Is that a gun?"

He doesn't respond. Instead, he kind of clucks; as though his Adam's apple has turned into a peach stone and all future swallows will be accompanied by this hollow, wooden sound effect.

I say, "Dad, is that a gun?"

You can feel the heat of the room curling between your eyelashes.

"Dad . . ."

The gun is clutched between his hands now, its nose pointed at my throat. The hole like a little iron nostril. I am exhausted. My ribs ache. To tell you the truth, I actually don't care very much.

His fury has a smell. Like undercooked pork. Cold, undercooked pork.

In a slow, deliberate lean the gun gets closer and closer. It's as if the gun has suddenly animated autogenously and the science fiction of it all is leading his hands.

I am thinking, No, Dad. Please, no. But nothing comes out.

He says, "Don't move."

He says, "Don't move," as if there is a wasp crawling on my shoulder.

The gun is in my mouth now. The cylinder forcing my lips apart. Like kissing the engine of a toy train. Its smell of axle grease. Its weight incredible on my teeth. The taste cold and dumb and molecular.

My father seethes. His breath is hot and his skin is a flat dull pink and I don't recognize myself in him. I see nothing of his only son in this strange violent intimacy. The wide nose. A small, rectangular scar below his bottom lip. The far-spread eyes. The flesh under his chin forming a kind of fatty trestle at the top of his neck. His hair not graying but turning a womanish, chemical yellow. For some reason I have this thought that I am from a stork. I was birthed on a mountainside, flown to the suburbs by a mythological fowl, and dropped through the mouth of a chimney.

I hear my mother's voice.

"Earl," she says. "Put the gun down, Earl."

Her voice is gentle with fatigue.

"Not this way, honey."

It's as if she is coaxing a child out of a tree.

Not this way, honey.

What does that mean?

My father clucks again. And with this cluck, somehow I realize that his fury is not about my sister but, rather, that her death is a kind of flashpoint in the half-life of his dwindling vapor of sanity. The spark that has lit a crucible. The final crack in his undamming river of disappointments.

There's my mother. The even, priestlike register of her voice. Her fat arms and her one knee that sticks and the subtle hump in her back that has emerged like a swollen, tumorous parasite trying to escape the cold prison of her flesh. This utilitarian convenience that was once a marriage with passion or heat or enough of a strand of lust to permit their bodies to mingle in what was to be two acts of procreation. Their strange, sexless husbandry. His low-ceilinged career. The mortgage payments. The broken-down cars and the abortive kitchen gadgets. Toasters and can openers and Crockpots. The small woodshop that never got built in the garage. The cosmetic smell of spackling correcting the Sheetrock. Yards and yards of Sheetrock. Miles of blank white walls and their failed promise. The birdless birdhouse. The tree in the front yard always bleeding with its milky cancer. The predictable, humid Joliet summers. The snow-heaped winters whose windchill is a kind of biblical rectification. The rectory silence of dinner broken only by the TV or the clink of utensils on plates or the sob of a hated piano.

Play for us, Son. Play while your mother clears the table.

He would remove the gun from my mouth and my mother would take it and drop it in the trash, somehow rendering the thing powerless.

The taste of it still haunts me. Sickens me. You can suck on a penny and get pretty close.

I would eventually lift off the chair and walk out of our little blond house on Gael Drive. Tired. My ribs inflamed. I would lurch/slouch/spiral to a bus stop, my body moving with thoughtless locomotion, as if some sort of imperfect, homemade ratchet wrench. The bus would take me to the train station.

I take Amtrak as far east as it will go.

Having slept next to an enormous cutlery salesman from Teaneck, New Jersey, I would arrive in New York City the following morning in a kind of severe, tightly coiled body clench.

Grand Central Station. Commuters and merchants and runaways colliding in a kind of electron bombardment. A cathedral with noise. So many suits. Anonymity.

Here is where I would begin my fifteen-year disappearance from the town with the little blond house on Gael Drive. I would step out onto Forty-second Street with twelve dollars and forty-two cents in my pocket.

The hipbone is connected to the leg bone.

III

So your resilient narrator makes his way in New York City.
He gets a job at a used-book store in the East Village,
where the stacks lean and sway toward the ceiling like
something out of a Dr. Seuss story. He earns a modest wage
of seven dollars an hour. He rents a room from an old
woman he meets at the store — Mrs. Levitsky, a Nabokov
fanatic. She lives on Tenth Street between First Avenue and
Avenue A, next to a Russian and Turkish bathhouse, where
on a cool night the smell of eucalyptus drifts up from the
courtyard and in through the window to his 9-by-9 room.
There is a naked bulb burning from the center of the
ceiling, a watercolor of an old man playing a banjo framed
on the inside of the door, and a small childlike twin
mattress on the floor that affords about the same quality of
comfort as a folded raincoat.

He has books. One of the perks from the store. Anything
he wants as long as it's not signed or rare. He uses the

books like bricks. He makes literary furniture. He builds a small table beside his bed where he keeps his wallet and his watch.

The Tin Drum, Out of Africa, A Moveable Feast.

The titles are a kind of dull horizontal comfort.

Light in August, The Grapes of Wrath, Tender Is the Night.

With more books he erects what appears to be a sloping, saddle-backed credenza, on which he lays out his four pairs of socks, his two pairs of pants, his three shirts, his six pairs of underwear, an unbreakable comb, and a fifty-cent canvas belt he buys off a malarial sheet on Second Avenue.

The Catcher in the Rye, The House of Mirth, A Gun for Sale.

After he gets on his feet, he purchases a used manual typewriter from a thrift store on First Avenue. A 1954 Underwood portable. Roughly the size of a coffee cake. Its manual return sounds like a great zipping slingshot. He uses more books to build a work desk.

Giovanni's Room, Sentimental Education, Ulysses.

He secures the desk with twine. The Underwood has a home.

For Whom the Bell Tolls, A Frolic of His Own, She Came to Stay.

He would stare at the typewriter as though it was some sort of singing tropical fish. He would wait for it to break into song for roughly two years.

But he reads his head off. Literature proves to be a great escape. Don DeLillo. James Baldwin. Dorothy Allison. Cormac McCarthy. J. D. Salinger. Gertrude Stein. Hemingway and Fitzgerald. Haruki Murakami. William Faulkner. Carol Shields. Günter Grass. Carson McCullers. William Gaddis. John Steinbeck. Simone de Beauvoir. Kenzaburo Ōe. Jane and Paul Bowles. Camus. Joseph Conrad. Harper Lee. John Edgar Wideman. John Updike. Edith Wharton. Graham Greene. Michael Ondaatje.

The names alone are a kind of escape.

Eventually Mrs. Levitsky gives her lease up and moves to North Carolina to paint birds. She leaves her collection of Nabokov behind.

First editions of *Lolita, Pale Fire, Invitation to a Beheading.*

He finds a 900-square-foot apartment on St. Marks Place, where the rent is six hundred dollars a month. It's a low-ceilinged, funhouse-floored Skinner Box. He packs up his books and his Underwood portable typewriter and his clothes and his unbreakable comb, and he carries the small parts of his life the two blocks south as if he is portaging a ruined canoe through a Canadian ice storm.

The former tenant leaves him a box of baking soda in the refrigerator, a roll of aluminum foil in a cupboard, and a small iron pot on the stove. In the middle of the kitchen there is a claw-footed bathtub, where, nightly, he would wash himself and then his clothes. He would hang his small, sopping wardrobe on a line of twine he'd string across the kitchen, where the clothes would drip-dry on the linoleum floor like a perpetual evening rain.

He sleeps on the floor.

He finds a chair on the street that sits pretty even if he keeps the *Book Review* of the *Times* folded under one of its legs.

The public toilet is on the floor below. So voiding his bowels turns into an act of gastrointestinal performance art.

He dines at Habib's Palace on Ninth Street between First and A. For two dollars there's falafel in a pita, complete with cucumber, black olives, onion, lettuce, tabouli, chickpeas, a mild jalapeño pepper, and fresh tomatoes.

He discovers ramen. He learns all the secrets. The right amount of broth to leave in. The cheap things to add. Scallions. Mushrooms. Chopped garlic. He is the Ramen Noodle King of St. Marks Place.

The bookstore gives him a dollar raise. He saves enough money to buy a set of cafeteria plates. A pair of forks. A spoon. A knife. A few more shirts. Eventually a table. A dresser. A kind of library hutch where his books find salvation from their improper utility as bricks. He dismantles his literary ensemble of credenza, work desk, and bedside table.

In the Skin of a Lion, The Sheltering Sky, Hard-Boiled Wonderland and the End of the World.

He eats. He sleeps. He voids his bowels.

The bookstore has poetry readings on Saturday nights, where he sits and listens.

He buys a futon. During the day it doubles as a sofa, where he spends most of his time reading.

His small apartment with the bathtub in the center of the kitchen fills with more books.

White Noise, A Confederacy of Dunces, Rabbit Run.

The nights turn into days. The days to weeks. Summer to fall. Rain to snow.

A few years pass.

He's promoted to assistant manager at the bookstore, which means he gets to lock up at night.

One day the Underwood calls to him. Your narrator goes to it. He rolls in two sheets of paper. He starts to type. It feels like an instrument. He composes. It flies out of his fingers. Although there is no sheet music, he writes a symphony of machine-gun staccato; a novel about a Midwestern guy who accidentally kills his little sister in an automobile accident. He is a former piano protégé and an insomniac. After his father sticks a gun in his mouth, the protagonist turns, walks out of the house, takes a train to

New York City, and never looks back. The protagonist has trouble connecting to people. The story sounds vaguely familiar.

He begins reading chapters of the novel at the Saturday-evening poetry readings. He gets feedback. Mostly positive. He gains confidence.

At one of the poetry readings, after his weekly chapter, a beautiful redheaded girl with gray-green eyes asks him if he'd be interested in joining her for a beer.

He hesitates. Her eyes are like Hemingway's Caribbean Sea.

"No," he says. "I'm sorry."

She gives him her phone number anyway.

The Caribbean Sea haunts him.

One day he calls her and they get together for a beer. She is originally from Michigan. She's an actress. When she's not using American stage speech, their A's sound similar. They laugh at the way they say "family" or "Saturday" or "jam." When she smiles, something inside him turns into music.

They meet several times, and something in your narrator awakens. They discuss his novel. They discuss her acting career. They take long walks and sit in the park and read aloud to each other.

The redheaded girl with the gray-green eyes gives his novel to a friend who knows a friend who has a friend at a prominent publishing house. The novel is passed on to an editor who has a reputation for taking risks. Surprisingly, the novel is bought after one read. What luck. What unbelievable luck. Agentless, he is paid a whopping advance of seven thousand, five hundred dollars. A literary fairy tale.

Life is good.

So, your resilient narrator and the redheaded girl with the gray-green eyes go out to celebrate. They get a little drunk. She invites him back to her place on Ninth Street between Broadway and University. He sits in her room and watches her undress. She is a beautiful flower opening to him. He undresses, too, and after several tender minutes of kissing and touching and holding each other, your narrator discovers that he is unable to attain an erection.

They meet the following night and try again. They put music on. They slow-dance. They exchange hot-oil massages. She attempts fellatio, only to be faced with the same flaccid result.

This goes on for approximately three weeks. The redheaded girl with the gray-green eyes who helped him publish his novel is unbelievably understanding. After a while she accepts his impotence and assures him that it doesn't even matter.

But he can't bear the humiliation. The sea will crush you if you don't know how to swim.

Eventually, they stop seeing each other. She calls him for a few weeks. He doesn't return her calls. Something inside him has died. Inexplicably. Rivers dry up and turn into garbage dumps. This is the image he sees: a virginal, fish-infested garbage dump.

So it's back to his apartment with the bathtub in the center of the kitchen. Back to his books and his laundry and his nightly linoleum rain.

Back to his various modes of escape and survival. Because you have to escape to survive, as you must survive to escape.

Despite getting some very nice reviews in *Publishers Weekly* and two other small trade journals, his novel sells modestly. It sells less than two thousand copies, to be exact.

He reads and rereads everything he owns. His own history turns into a kind of amorphous passage of words. Time flattens and distorts into text: his own and the great literary monuments of others. Chapters are months. Authors seasons.

Let It Come Down, The Power and the Glory, Another Country.

The books turn into years. The years into books. The Underwood stops calling to him.

He periodically dreams of music. Flying pianos playing themselves. Enormous but as light as beach balls. Pianos turning into horses. Giant World War II Steinways lining the middle of First Avenue; taxis slaloming backwards between their legs and disappearing skyward at Houston Street.

Grieg. Chopin. Tchaikovsky.

He wakes from these dreams with an ache. A kind of cold intestinal sorrow.

One day, fifteen years later, your resilient narrator gets a flat manila envelope addressed by his father. Inside there is no letter. Only a rather grainy Xerox of a short story, written in longhand, dated December 2, 1949.

(He removes a folded manila envelope from his back pocket, takes out the story, reads.)

THE STORY OF MY LIFE

I was born on November 8, 1940, at 1:45 a.m. at Grant Hospital, Chicago, Illinois. When I was one I grabbed a hot-water pipe and burned my hand. Three months later I was in a Baby Photograph Contest. My picture was put in the newspapers, even though I didn't have any hair 'cause of a fever. I was pretty bald, but I was holding a tomato.

When I was three I went to the park and climbed the ladder to the slide all by myself. When I went for my turn, a bigger boy pushed me and I cut my lower lip. It took about a month to heal and this one dog called Big Steve always

licked my cuts. My mother said that was good
'cause dogs have the cleanest tongues in Western
Civilization. It left a scar. I still have the scar.

I started school at four years old. My teacher
had a metal hand. In homeroom we had to take
a nap. I always woke up with waffles on my
face.

Then we lived in Diamond Lake for three years
and several months. There was a haunted house in
this field behind our garage. One day me and my
boy friend Tony Wood were throwing rocks at the
apple trees. These cows were grassing and then
they smelled some gum that was stuck to Tony
Wood's shoe. They started chasing us, so we ran to
the other field and climbed a windmill. The cows
really wanted the gum. We were so scared we
started yelling at the cows. Tony Wood was yelling
"The Star-Spangled Banner" 'cause he said the
Army would come if you yelled that, but I was just
yelling. The cows wanted to murder us and take
the gum, but they finally went away after Tony
Wood sang "The Butler's Got a Headache, Don't
Give Him Any Cheese." He was real scared, but he
sang it good 'cause he was in choir.

My mother used to work as a waitress and now she still is a waitress. My father used to be a chef and now he works at the post office and paints pictures of ducks in the garage.

One winter I was pulling Tony Wood on a sled and we fell in the ice. We helped each other out and we went over to his house because it was the closest to the lake. I didn't get ammonia, but I couldn't swallow anything that night. Tony Wood didn't get ammonia either, but his hand turned blue.

When I grow up I want to be a fireman, policeman, or a soldier. Each one of those men plays an important part for our country. A policeman catches crooks, leads children across the street, and etc. A fireman puts out fires, helps cats out of trees, and etc. A soldier fights for his country, guards the President, and etc. That's why I want to be one of those men when I grow up.

My Uncle Hy is my greatest influence. He teaches me how to build pinewood derby cars, he helps me with my verbs, he takes me to track meets, we play Ping Pong, and etc. That is why he is my greatest influence.

Attached to the back of the story there is a small letter-sized white envelope.

(He reveals the envelope.)

Your narrator opens the envelope. Inside there is a note card.

(He opens the envelope, holds up the note card.)

It reads:

> Son,
> I have been diagnosed with testicular cancer. I
> don't have much longer to live. Please come home.
> Love,
> Dad

Clipped to the note card are two crisp one-hundred-dollar bills.

(He turns the note card around, reveals the money.)

And a P.S.

Please use the money to help you get here.

At the bottom of the note card, in blue pencil, your resilient narrator's father's new address is printed with childlike, strained perfection.

IV

So I take Amtrak from New York to Chicago's Union Station. There's a cold Lake Michigan wind that makes the ten-minute walk to the LaSalle Street station feel like a kind of ruthless, pedestrian damnation. I wait twenty minutes or so and get the Metra Rock Island line south to Joliet.

I walk from the train station.

The wind again. Cold as Novocain. As if Lake Michigan has packaged its brutality and sold it to smaller, lakeless river towns.

Fifteen years later Joliet hasn't changed. The iron sky. The skin of the river weltering with the hairy shafts of rotted trees and neglected picnic tables and the corpses of cars. The horizon so low you can look out and almost see the earth bulging on its axis. The harsh black fields beyond the city limits.

The only difference is a casino boat anchored on the river. It looks like an enormous wedding cake buoyed to the canal. There are no decks and the windows are mirrored, as if they were rummaged from a midtown office-building auction. Its white frosted body gives it the air of a warship in drag.

My father's second-floor apartment overlooks the river. There's an old, rusted train bridge where enormous black birds nest. It is late fall, and the water underneath the bridge is molecular and gray and choked with October-hardened cattails that clatter in the breeze as if they have been whittled slender from the brittle bones of animals.

I knock on the door. There is no answer. The lamp in the hall is broken and the evening's last bit of sunlight has settled into the stairwell the way a familiar smell settles into an old chair. I knock again. I wait. Still no answer. I open the door. There is a stench. Something intestinal. A kind of damp fecal rot.

My father is asleep in an old La-Z-Boy recliner. There is a color TV on the floor in front of him. The sound is turned down and the screen is casting a strange blue light on his face. His weight loss is tremendous. The eyes sunken. The double chin gone. There is a small patch of yellowish-gray hair tufting from his skull. A post-chemical fur that looks as if it has not taken root but, rather, alighted and spread like some kind of airborne viral moss. His mouth is open. His teeth a grayish milky blue.

There is an agony around his eyes. Somehow he looks as if he is not sleeping but affecting a kind of calorie-conserving, geriatric inertia prescribed to keep death at bay.

The Steinway is wedged into the corner like an enormous black gland. It looks as new and as old as it was fifteen years ago. On top of the bench a copy of my novel: the title just a smear of text in the half-light. I can't fathom how he got the piano into the apartment, but it's there in all its hulking omnipotence, as though it willed itself to levitate and fly in through the window.

Paneling has been pressed over the plastered walls; the kind of infinitely grooved paneling that warps and chafes with a sinister eczema.

Toward the back of the apartment a buckling electric hospital bed. Its position in the room is as arbitrary as a chaise lounge on a windblown beach. The linens are twisted into harsh braids over the plastic ticking.

A space heater has been set a few feet to the left of the La-Z-Boy.

I close the door and just stand there for a long time. I watch my father. Fifteen years warrants a melodramatic pause. An actor's moment.

There's a kindness in his sleep. A compassion in the agony around his eyes.

I have an impulse to eat. Prodigal son returns home. Prodigal son is so poor he didn't want to squander his money in the café car and he wants a sandwich. I cross to the kitchenette and open a small refrigerator that looks more like something you use for the storage of fishing supplies. Inside, there are three tubs of cottage cheese, a gallon of milk, some strange, medicinal ointments in silver tubes, and a small Tupperware container of what appears to be chunks of liver.

I hear, "There's a six-pack of Coors in the crisper."

My father's voice sounds as if it has been cut in half.

"Had the new hospice guy pick it up for me this afternoon. His name is Jerry, I think. Is it there?"

"Yeah, it's there," I say. "Want one?"

"No, thank you," he says.

I grab a Coors from the crisper and close the refrigerator. In the distance I can hear a train approaching; the final inbound Metraliner from Chicago.

He says, "No bags, huh?"

I say, "I wasn't planning a long visit."

My free hand is wedged deep into my pocket.

He says, "Take your coat off."

I say, "Sure."

But I don't take it off.

"That might have been your last train. You're more than welcome to stay."

"Thanks," I say. "Maybe just a night or so."

"There's an inflatable mattress in the closet."

The light has been left on in the bathroom. For some reason I feel the need to turn it off. I cross the kitchenette and open the bathroom door. There is a metal orthopedic walker in front of the toilet. Above the sink a handprint on the mirror. Perhaps my father's. A kind of strained recognition. My reflection is feeble and yellow. My eyes red with fatigue. A cross-country train's capacity to age you. I turn the light off and head back out.

"How do you like the digs?" he asks. He coughs before I can answer. It sounds as if something has torn in his lung. "It was a former button-making shop."

"It's nice," I say, taking a slug of beer. "About the size of my place."

"The hospital has a shuttle bus that picks me up on the corner for my treatments. It's convenient."

I picture him getting on and off a shuttle bus. Does he use the walker? How does he get down the stairs? The thought makes me tired.

"Sit over there," he says, pointing to the piano bench. "Where I can see you."

"I'll just sit here on the floor," I say, pointing to a spot a safe distance from the Steinway.

For some reason I'm not able to sit.

I say, "Maybe I'll stand for a minute."

I notice the morphine cartridge that has been intravenously fed into the underside of his right arm. He clutches a small trigger plunger. I have this absurd vision of him pressing the plunger and being ejected from the La-Z-Boy. The afflicted daredevil. He flies through the window circus-like, somersaults into a full gainer, and lands in the river.

"How was your trip?" he asks.

"Fine," I say. "I took the train."

"Quite a ways."

"Seventeen hours," I say. "Lots of old people."

"Someone pick you up from the station?" he asks.

I say, "I walked."

He says, "I could've had Jerry—"

"It's okay," I say.

"He uses the old Fleetwood."

I say, "Thanks, Dad. It's just that cars . . . Even being in one."

He says, "Of course."

I tell him how in New York I can't even get in a taxi.

He says, "I understand, Son."

My free hand is still fisted in my pocket, as if I am concealing a stone.

I say, "Thanks for the money. I don't think I would have been able to come if—"

He holds his hand up to stop me, and with this gesture I understand that my father's suffering periodically induces the need to be wordless; to use a kind of restrained pantomime. Something priestlike. A silent Hosanna.

I ask him if he's in a lot of pain, and he says that it comes and goes, and he showcases the morphine cartridge.

"They give me free rein with it now," he says.

The light is fading on the window. The skin of the river is black. Moonlight is marbling under the bridge strange and silver.

"I read your book," he says, gesturing toward my novel on the piano bench as if it is a sleeping child.

I say, "Yeah, I saw it over there."

He says, "Got through it in two sittings."

"I'm glad," I say.

"Fella from the *Herald News* ran a review of it. Said some nice things. The bookstore over on Center Street had a few copies, but they sold them all. Said they couldn't reorder it for some reason."

I say, "It's out of print."

"Well, it shouldn't be," he says. He coughs and then says it again.

Well, it shouldn't be.

It's the nicest thing he's ever said to me.

He adds, "You write very well," and then he presses the button on his morphine plunger, doesn't eject, and says, "The section about the accident . . ." His head drops back a bit. He settles into the La-Z-Boy. "In the book the guy just keeps going as if he was guilty of some—"

"It's a novel, Dad. It's fiction."

He says, "Of course."

I say, "I took liberties."

Then we are quiet for a moment. He is looking at me with a kind of sorrowful hunger. His mouth collapsed. His eyes heavy with that historical anguish. As though I am his executioner with the power to pardon. I am suddenly seized with the need to leave. I can stay at the YMCA. I start for the door.

He says, "You're losing your hair, huh?"

I stop.

I say, "So are you."

"Fuzz doesn't count," he says.

I turn back. "Sorry," I say. "Bad joke."

He smiles. His teeth again. Dim as a once-bitten apple.

He says, "They say a son gets his hair from his mother."

I say, "Jan had some intense hair."

"It was thin as a Kleenex," he says. "You wouldn't have known it, though, with all the crap she put in it."

"Do you keep in touch with her?" I ask.

"Not so much anymore," he says. "We used to write."

I say, "She still at the home?"

He says, "Yeah, she's still there. It's where she feels safe."

I take a few more steps toward the middle of the room and ask if he misses her.

"Do you miss her?" I ask.

He says, "Used to. Not so much anymore."

"Have you had other relationships?"

"No," he says. "None. Not a one in fifteen years."

We're quiet again. As the room darkens, the TV takes on a campfire quality. The infectious blue light. Even the window a deep cobalt now. My father has hardly moved. I realize that I'm still standing.

He says, "She used to ask about you a lot. If I'd heard from you. I used to tell her you wrote me."

"What did I write?" I ask.

He says, "You wrote that you were in the Army. That you were in school studying chemistry. That you got married in Virginia. I'd make stuff up."

I don't respond. Something has thickened in me. Sediment. The remains of some unknown solid not eaten but breathed in during a moment of weakness or shame. A bloodless stone in my throat.

I say, "I think I should leave."

He says, "Don't leave."

I say, "This doesn't feel right."

He says, "Please don't leave, Son," and then he starts to cry. He cries silently and into the hand holding the plunger. Like a child with a toy. Perhaps there is a poem or a saying that gets you through these moments of bitterness. A kind of hymn or Jesus song. I wait for a softening.

"Please don't leave me," he says again. And we are quiet.

After your father has cried in front of you for the first time, the silence in the room is like an orchestra raising their instruments, waiting for the conductor's baton to cue the beginning of a symphony.

"Can I get you something?" I ask.

He says, "Maybe some water."

I cross to the kitchenette, grab a clean glass out of the cupboard, and fill it with tap water. When I return, he has shifted the La-Z-Boy out of its recline. His legs are white and hairless and birdlike. I hand him the water. He drinks the entire glass and hands it back.

As I'm setting the glass in the sink, he says, "I used to dream about her every night."

I say, "Mom?"

He says, "No. Your sister."

"That must have been hard," I say.

"Simple things. Sitting at the kitchen table. Seeding the bird feeder. The dreams ended about five years ago."

I don't say anything. The wind can be heard coming through the caulking. Like a small cat bawling. I cross to the window and put my hand on the pane. It's cold and damp.

My father says, "I like the title of your novel. An homage to Grieg."

I sit.

" 'Nocturne' was your best competition piece," he says. "Do you still play?"

"No," I say. "I don't."

He says, "That's too bad."

I'm still wearing my coat. I take it off and fold it over my arm.

He says, "I just had the Steinway tuned again last month. I've been trying to play a bit myself, but I'm just a hack. 'Chopsticks.' 'Yankee Doodle Dandy.' "

He laughs again. I rise and cross to the window. On the river the casino boat has lit up garishly. It has an air of evangelism now, as though it is not being powered by fuel or coal but, rather, by an enormous fire-blown pipe organ and a holy choir.

He asks, "Did you read my story?"

"I did," I say. " 'The Story of My Life.' Great title."

"I thought you might find it amusing."

I say, "I was moved by its honesty."

I sit again and drink from the Coors, which is warm and aluminum-tasting now. My other hand has finally emerged from my pocket and it's making small dents in the can.

"So do you have any romance in your life?" he asks. "A girlfriend?"

"No," I say. "Not really."

"Handsome fella like yourself?"

I tell him I was seeing someone for a while, but that it didn't work out.

He says, "Why not?"

"Because I'm impotent," I say. It's as if I've said, "Because I weigh a hundred and fifty-five pounds" or "Because I like pepperoni pizza." A harmless biographical fact. And then I add, "I've never really been with a woman, Dad."

He says, "All these years?"

"I'm a thirty-two-year-old virgin."

And then he completely surprises me and asks me if I'm a homosexual.

He says, "Are you a homosexual?"

I say, "No." I say, "No, I'm not a homosexual. At least I don't think so."

He says, "Plenty of ladies out there. Especially in New York City."

I say, "I just don't do very well with people."

He gives me a little fatherly advice. He says, "It takes time."

I say, "An impotent virgin isn't a very good combination. Plus, I work at a bookstore. I'm not exactly made of money. Not the greatest résumé in the world."

"Women fall for poets all the time," he says.

I tell him about the redheaded girl with the gray-green eyes who helped me publish my novel. I narrate our courtship and the time we spend reading aloud to each other and our walks along the park. I romanticize her Caribbean Sea eyes and the intensity with which she listens and her laugh that awakened me.

I look up and I realize that my father has fallen asleep. What sentence, I wonder. During what drop in my voice?

His mouth is wide open and a small snore is catching in his throat, barely audible. I can't imagine navigating through that kind of pain medication. The morphine lulling you to sleep. That syrupy warmth. Like a lover's whisper pulling you under.

I grab the quilt off his bed, gently shift the La-Z-Boy back into its recline, and cover him. My father smells of urine and his breath is baked with a chemical burn, and up close his skin has a rubbery, almost industrial quality. But despite the vomit stains from chemotherapy and the toxicity of his breath and his toddlerlike incontinence, I take his hand. It is long and slender and soft like a woman's.

The hand of a pianist.

I stay there like that for a long time.

The blue light from the TV continues to fill the room. For several hours I sit next to the La-Z-Boy and watch anonymous men and women moving their mouths in a kind of silent, meaningless purgatory.

My father doesn't shift in the chair once. He hardly breathes. He simply is. Painlessly. Almost pleasantly. His fingers curled around my hand as though I am silently leading him around the ice rink.

Through the window I can see that it has started to snow. The flakes are enormous and they fall with a stillness attributed to hawks and seagulls. The blue-stained snow framed in the window light. Finding white again as it feathers across the pane.

"It's snowing," I say. I know he can't hear me, but I say it again. "It's snowing, Dad."

EPILOGUE

My father died that night.

When Jerry arrived the following morning with his hospice supplies, he cleaned the room and called in the death and packed up my father's few possessions. When he woke me, I was asleep on the floor next to the La-Z-Boy, my father's hand still grasped in mine.

Jerry said that my father was day-to-day and that they were surprised he had made it through the fall. He said it was good that I had come. That it probably helped my father let go.

There was a small memorial service in a grotto behind a chapel that I had never seen before. My mother was not in attendance. I didn't recognize anyone and I doubt that anyone recognized me. It snowed and it was cold and very few spoke on his behalf, but those who did said he was a fine man who did great things for the school district and the children at Monge Junior High School.

He chose to be cremated, and his ashes were stuffed into a small pinewood box that some anonymous school district colleague signed for at the funeral home.

Jerry was kind enough to offer me a ride to the train station, but although I told him I was grateful, I had to refuse. I walked to Union Station in the snow, caught the Metraliner north to Chicago and the overnight Amtrak east to Grand Central Station wearing the same clothes I had departed in.

My father left me four thousand dollars and the Steinway. For thirty-five dollars a month I keep the Steinway in storage back in Joliet. Perhaps someday I will play it again. Perhaps I'll sell it.

The other day I called the redheaded girl with the gray-green eyes. We are going to meet again sometime very soon. She told me she missed me. I told her I had so much to tell her.

Even the greatest sleeping sea can be awakened by the tide.

Grief does not expire like a candle or the beacon on a lighthouse. It simply changes temperature. It becomes a kind of personal weather system. Snow settles in the liver. The bowels grow thick with humidity. Ice congeals in the stomach. Frost spiderwebs in the lungs. The heart fills with warm rain that turns to mist and evaporates through a colder artery.

Sometimes when I can't sleep I'll walk up the east side of First Avenue. A cabby naps in the back seat of his double-parked taxi. A Ukrainian woman cleans a fish at the counter of her darkened diner. A Dominican man sitting in the entrance to the butcher's stares out at nothing in particular, his eyes black as burnt stones.

I am continually amazed by the 5 a.m. silence that is possible in New York. The streetlights infinitesimally swaying as though bored. That flattened hour when, in some barren, half-dreamed lot, even the cars seem to be sleeping.

I cross to the west side of First Avenue at Twenty-third Street. A fellow insomniac is reading a paperback in the window of an all-night diner. This is where I turn around and walk home on the opposite side of the street; past the Italian bakery and the hospital with its silent, sliding doors, and the Korean deli at Thirteenth Street where a small Mexican boy cuts flowers and sprays down the sidewalk.

I reach St. Mark's Place and cross back to the east side of First Avenue. With a kind of recovered peace I climb the four flights of stairs and return to my apartment with the bathtub in the kitchen.

My sister.

My father.

My mother sleepwalking in a cotton hospital dress.

(The distant sound of Grieg's "Nocturne" can be heard.)

Stars.

Moonlight.

A black field full of snow.

How many breaths do you take in a night?

The Underwood still calls to me.

Still calls to me through the rich, oblivious darkness.